A Butterfly's Love:

What one can't imagine, can happen

CARMEN GONZALEZ

ISBN: 978-1-09835-992-8 (paperback)
ISBN: 978-1-09835-993-5 (ebook)

Acknowledgements

I would like to thank my eldest son Anthony L. Johnson Jr, for his persistence in making sure his drawing depicts the meaning I desired to portray. Anthony drew and designed my cover page, thank you so much. To Solomon, Samuel, Isaiah and Josiah Johnson, sons thank you for your diligence in making sure I was not stressed out at the end of the day. Thank you for taking charge and doing what was needed to be done. To my mother Carmen Santiago, who always asked "How is your book coming along?" Thank you, mama, for ensuring that I never gave up. To my father Hiram Gonzalez, I want to say that every day you made sure to tell me "Trust no one but God", "this is your season". Pops I receive that, and I believe that. Thank you so much! An abundance of love to my sisters Sandra Gonzalez, Elisa Brown, Abigail Couzens, Rebecca Baylis, and to my brother Hiram Gonzalez. You provided me with great advice and encouraged me during the entire process. You made sure that the best decision was made. To my most devoted supporter and encourager, my friend, my everything, Claude Troupe. Thank you for insisting that I go ahead and publish my poetry. Thank you for the long nights of going over each piece, line by line; and providing feed back. To my best friend, my sister, Bernadette Lee, I appreciate you, and thank you for always being there, and being patient with me. To Krystal Cureton, my sister, every time I spoke with you, your words echoed into my spirit. "You got this sis, you got this, so proud of you". Thank you for your support. To everyone who is going to support, by purchasing a book or providing encouragement, Thank you!

CONTENTS

A Woman's Fight

Introduction

It's always hard to express one's inner emotions and flow with no distraction. The biggest mistake many make, is doubting themselves. Poetry for me is a way to release my emotions that boils inside. I encourage my readers to find a place of peace and release your inner thoughts. Whether in writing poetry or songs, whether dancing or drawing, find that one thing that releases all tension and allows you to float. As you read each piece, I ask that you read from the heart. Allow each piece to draw you in as if you have put it together. Whether you are in love, in a relationship hoping to fall in love; or you are a mother whose heart wants the best for her children; or perhaps you have sisters who really encourage you and push you; a brother that loves you for you; a family that really cares and has your back; or finally whether you have gone through some things that you hold bondage in your heart. Feel each word, each line in fact; allow it to penetrate to the core of your heart. Its ok to shed a tear or two; perhaps grab a pillow and release the scream within. Freeing yourself of the pain allows for a balance in life.

Each topic is designed with purpose and ambition; designed to cover the area in a woman's life that really mean the world to her. Women wear so many hats and at times we find it easier to do for others then to take care of our own desires. Women consume so many emotions and feelings that at the end of the day a glass of wine and music, helps it all go away. Join me in this journey of emotions and satisfaction, and really releasing the things that kept me in bondage.

Endless Love Awaits

Indefinite

My handsome king, what can I say, I am in love with you so desperately; your arms is where I want to be. Your kiss is what I desire the most. Your warm hugs so powerful and inviting; covering me and securing me. Your strong touch with the towel above; I cling to you, for my safe haven you have become. Man, of my dreams you have not let me down, you have proven yourself so honestly. You have given me a sense of constant love, no doubt at all. I love you my king for being unique; I love you my king for being you, in every way possible.

Passionate

Desired to be held, crippled by the moment. A life time of love enclosed within; so deeply rooted, I never knew. Captured by truth, illuminated by the fear that this love over takes me. Out runs me from within and camps all night. A love so strong prisoned by this emotion I have become; left wanting more, trapped with the few. To stand, to breath, I just want you. Nothing else matters, your love is all so true. You've captured my heart and taken my life with you. You've combined our lives with these emotions so strong; amazingly amazing this thing called love. I wouldn't change it, not even for a second; I wouldn't hand it back over to you for a moment. My entire being, my love is wrapped in you; for once in my life I have experienced this so true. Fingers through my lips, just one more kiss, hands over my face a gentle touch resides. I am vulnerable with you, so comfortable yet scared. I am ready to let go of myself and give you my all. Cherish me my dear, for fragile I am; I am a precious jewel I've waited so long its true. Please tread these waters lightly, please cover me above. Protect me my king and love me wholeheartedly.

Captured

Ambition, hope, and growth, all driven by love, not taken as joke. Abandoned the past, the pain released; newness has come and brought a new found growth within. Escaping, the words muttered by most; leaping by faith into uncharted territory. It's strength that has kept me thus far you know, its love that brought me another day above. I am grateful, I am yours, I am content in wanting more. What is this thing everyone fights about, who is this man I have fallen hard for? Climbing never stopping above, I want to go further, to swim in this alone. Escaping to your arms forever will be, to cherish, to hold, til death do us part.

Buttered up

Love is a word that carries a lot of responsibilities; it is supposed to take the hurts and pains away and replace them with security and protection. Love speaks volumes when done from the heart; because true love doesn't hurt; instead, it wraps its arms around the love one. Love conditions and interacts with compassion and with care. Love for me isn't just a word any longer, instead it wraps itself in action, which creates a safe haven for both. Love never takes for granted nor does it get comfortable; love takes work and patience and appreciation. True love is handled with fragile cargo to ensure that the one we love never goes anywhere. Loves takes compromise and understanding on both sides. True love will conquer what hatred will never; true love will last beyond all other, when anger let's go!

Enchanted

Its so easy to love when you demonstrate love in so many ways. From the words you speak to the touch you give; to the kiss you share and the passion in making love. It's so easy to love when you cherish me and respect me and treat me like the queen I am. You caress me and take caution with me; you understand how fragile I am and you love me in spite of. You demonstrate to me what a queen really is, it goes further then just the word and the looks. You have given me the understanding that I myself, am a strong individual full of wisdom and worth. You have accepted my decisions, and taken into account. My silliness and energy have been understood; the love I have for the things I do; you have proven to accept. What I wear is up to me and judgment never comes out of your mouth; my walk has never been so profound; my confidence grows and in love so close. Speaking to you hours on the phone allows me to grow closer to you. Its so easy to love you when you listen to even the worst hurt in my life; you desire to protect me at all cost, even though your limited with that inside. Its so easy to love you, for you have created a safe haven for me and wrapped your arms around me instead of on me. Loving you has been the best feeling and comfort a woman can experience.

Addicted

Love so strong, it sweeps me off my feet causing me to whisper words I wouldn't before. It has me desiring this one so strong; how could this be, this love so real? I think of him always, just to know that he is near. When I hear his voice so clear, my heart begins to skip a beat, my stomach flutters like the birds outside. When I am with him, I stare at him in disbelief that this one person has caused me to feel this way.

Love so strong it sweeps me off my feet, causing my mind to spin all day and whisper his name for sure. In his presence I desire to be, no moment to soon, just let me be. His touch brings out the softness I have never felt; inside of me, I melt. When his lips reach mine, my body screams silently in desire. As we kiss my stomach tightens up, my mind can't comprehend all I feel. My defensive walls come up; for I cannot believe all of this. Love has me doing things I never dared to before. I am frightened by this love that deepens each day. I try to let go completely but fear tells me to be careful. If not cautious, love may hurt, if not patient it will be lost, if not affectionate it can be crazy. Who am I kidding, I can not live without this one, my heart takes control so easily and reminds me of the time we had together. In his arms I'd rather be, protected and safe knowing my life is easier with him.

Love so strong, it sweeps me off my feet; sleepless nights all because I desire him. Could love really be as strong and hard as I feel? Is it possible for my heart to deepen as the days progress? Man, I need him, his voice, touch, kiss, and arms. I need to feel calm again, for all over the place I feel. I need to step into my place as his lady I will be. This love right here keeps me going, strong and new, keeps me pressing forward and being that queen, I always knew I am.

Floating

I love you for what you represent, an image for all men to walk and model. The patience you have displayed have really encouraged me. Your loving arms which embraced and gave my heart shelter in the time of need. My love draws closer to me and carry me through allow me to be the woman I have always been destined to be. Never remove your love from me for in your arms my safety remains. I have never felt secured in a man; I have never allowed my walls to fall. It is with you that all of me comes through; my happiness flourishes and blossoms, my life will never be the same again. I love you my king, my man, my everything.

Content

I am happy, so content; I am full of joy and peace inside. I have met my mate, the love of my life, the one that causes my heart to skip a beat or two. His voice so perfect which draws me closer, his touch so warm and pleasant, I drown inside. His every stroke raises the temperature inside of me. His stroke causes me to desire him more. Words of wisdom, comfort and love he speaks to me. Fills me with love and cause me to faint. I am in love with him you see, from the bottom of my heart to the top of my mind. I will cherish him and keep him close and cause him to love me even more.

Moment times

I have never met a man so real, who doesn't mind showing his emotion. Its so rare to have a man who would talk a day away and would not get tired of his mate. A man who is concerned with not just his well being but the well being of his love. Conversations, laughter, stillness, reserve; I can not ask for anything more then the understanding you extend to me. You are so perfect in our own way, to listen, to lend a helping hand. It is not by chance that our paths have crossed; it is meant to be for you to guide me. A man with so much experience who doesn't mind waiting for the one thing a man desires the most. You make it about us and less about it; if I could be in your arms for one full day, I think I would melt away. You make me happy; you make me proud; you complete me from the inside out. Allow me to give you what you need, and in return you will not be disappointed. I need you my king whether you know it or not, I need you for eternity, for unconditional love you bring.

Love

Love is not defined by the people around us; it is not carried out by responsibilities. Instead, love is felt when two people are in tune to one another. When two people set aside their desires and needs to fulfill the others desire and needs. Love causes one to go above and beyond to do anything to please and satisfy that special one. To see a smile on their face; to hear laughter from them, love causes one to feel the pain, hurt and disappointments that our special one experiences. Love will guide you to each other's arm no matter who tries to set the two apart. Love never leads to a dead end, it always finds a path of safety and protection. It is my love that causes me to do what I need to do to be with you.

Patient love

Above the clouds to high to fly, floating in the air in disbelief. I have made my choice, my decision is final; I claim my prize, I take pleasure in you. I am proud of where we have come thus far, whose to tell our ending for sure; for our commitment to one another is far too great, our love outweighs all other. I am not one to give myself to many; I like to give my all to one. Two separate worlds we come from; however, what we have no one can maintain. We have established a relationship unheard of. The best of both worlds has finally met. Together we make a hell of a team, but separate we need each other desperately. We complete each other; make each other stronger. We are warriors at heart, no one will fully comprehend. We may tug, we may pull, at the end we always end up united. This wall we have built no one can tear down for its like no other wall ever built before. Don't fight my love against the truth, no longer keep me in the back too long. Beside you I belong for we are stronger like that. I plead my case my mind made up; its too late for you, for I have fallen hard over you. You can't release me or discharge me; I am here to stay whether you approve or not. Keep me near you, close by I must say. Its better that way for both our sake.

The kind of man a woman wants

Hard worker and dedicated to the cost; compassionate and patient; jumping hurdles to make one proud. Hands so rough because your job is never done; gentle touch provided that causes the butterflies to flutter. A man that has gone through some things and doesn't mind sharing the knowledge experienced. Words of encouragement given, for the tenderness inside him, comes out through his love. A real man indeed with expressions from the heart; one that doesn't mind sharing and perhaps going above and beyond for the cause of love. Arms so strong, muscles punctuate all around. The softness of his arms as he wraps his arms around a woman's body, causes her to faint and fall asleep, knowing that his arms are her safety and his love her comfort. Position for greatness, because he reaches that point, where he understands that his life is better when he lets go and allows a woman inside. The understanding given makes him most attractive and the unity he provides draws her inside. It's this type of man that every woman desire to have; and truth be told, he is out there waiting for you.

Strange

Is it strange that my love for you is so deep? Is it strange that I desire you in so many ways? My attachment only grows and deepens while my feelings cling to you. My heart gravitates to you and never steer me away from you. My mind is always thinking of the possibilities of a lifetime with you. My soul has settled within your life and mine. So, I ask is it strange that my love for you is so deep? Is it strange that I desire you in so may ways? Our souls connected, for life unknown this feeling becomes. We can be near or far but the fact remains that my love is yours. My body craves for you, all of you. Your all I want, all I need; you fulfill me, complete me and make me whole. Never cease getting to know me, never cease experimenting new things with me. Let's go above and beyond for one another and keep the fire burning; there is no question in my mind in regards to where we stand.

Balanced

What has become of true love if given up and throwing in the towel has succeeded, taken over for life. It raises a thought on whether true love really exist for by book, love is supposed to be unconditional; patient and caring. Love is understanding and not controlling. Love can not be bought but given freely just because. Love is so much more then meets the eye. Love is the combination of hurts, pain, acceptance, and most of all patients. Love has no judgement, it never looks down; rather love exiles above no other, love fights for rights and lays down its life for another. Love above anything else raises victorious and conquers the heart. So, what has become of true love if given up and throwing in the towel has succeeded.

A butterfly's love

Crawling and learning my way around the independent life one calls adulthood. Making sense of decisions that for one my age, both male and female would know for sure without a doubt, without hesitation. I have learned from mistakes and from my close family and friends. I have been wrapped and stuck in a bubble swirling out of control. What I thought I could of, I realize was much harder than anything imagined. Learning to fly and spread my wings, to live my life alone has been a challenge that keeps me confined within. I am not a robot, with knowledge beyond explanation, I am not a scientist with a mind so pure in design. I may not be a perfect butterfly with a background as most, but I am a woman who has survived many defects and adversary, that no one may never know. I am this woman with life full of joy, desiring to share this gift of love, unfamiliar to me but grateful to experience. My wings have broadened, my mind has expanded; no, I did not come to grips alone, but with the love that helped me through. I am only looking to move forward, higher, and deeper as I feel. This love I managed to experience, is only but new as if yesterday I experience it for the first time in life. It causes me to fly higher and allows me to feel deeper. I am flying out of control in this love that only grows each day. Is it fate? Is it purpose? Whatever it may be, I know for sure, that the feelings of love never vanish but grows deeper and wider. True love finds it way back to the heart, even when suppressed love must come forth. It is no game, no bother within; love is caring, warm and patient, never given up, never given in. What butterfly stops the purpose from its cycle from one stage to the next. This fine butterfly has managed to make it with my love beside me. I am willing to press through the good, through the bad, through the sickness, through the health. I will fly anywhere, from the butterfly to the love that makes the beauty evolve.

Product

We are the product of what we, yes, together have built. Our love has grown deeper than imagined, inseparable we have become. Although away from on another, our hearts are never too far apart.

We are the product of what we, yes, together have built. Nothing can hinder or even come close to tearing us apart. We have worked towards, and managed to complete each other. Not a day goes by that our love remains the same.

We are the product of what we, yes, together have built. As one, connected, bonded to a lifetime of our love.

Trapped

Perfect run for one that's desperate to go; all around are traps to stop the one from staying focus. Hard it is to maintain the purpose.; struggle gets deeper for the fight inside weakens. Who will run this race? Who will finish the course? Looking ahead, there is no end, but the trust comes in knowing that at the end, victory is won. Run far, run hard, run ahead without a detour; pick up the pace even when damage heads your way.

Perfect run for one that's desperate to go. Trapped by fear that easily creeps in; trying to decide whether or not the run would be worth the uncertainty. Away, it's been decided, I will run this race without any more hesitation, without any more doubt. Victory is mine at the end, I can sense it and with my pace, no time for me to arrive.

Never Stop A Mother's Love

A Mother's Love

Nine months it takes to develop the perfect one. A being with no care in the world; a being dependent on a mother's tube for food. The moment comes, the water breaks, it seems unbearable this pain at hand. The screams, the pushes, all gone when this tiny one takes a breath; when this tiny one gives a cry of relief. The first touch is so amazing, feels unreal that I have just birthed this tiny being. The notice of pain, gone completely and the joy of breath appears. In my arms finally, placed in my bosom for security. This tiny one now dependent on me, cries for my milk I must act quick. A little shiver, quiver, I must place a blanket on my tiny one. Protection comes with no sign, no instruction; I will be sure to give this being every-thing needed for survival and more. I will be everything to this tiny one until my years come to an end, and adulthood comes mama now steps back. Believe, that even though I have stepped back I will forever be around to catch this one; for a mother's love will never cease, never fade, even when the years pass away.

My life

Endless love I have for you, for the joy you bring me never compares to any experienced. My heart is full overtaken by you. Protection I give, extended love renewed. Every moment passes are one cher-ished with the core of you. For my boys, my young men, I admit you keep me balanced. My world you are and I will give my all for you to live a life full of gold. My hand is open never closed within. I give you me, my love, my soul. Surrounded by God's five perfection, living my life with everything I need and want. Completed by the hugs given, kisses provided, and good morning mom stated. Anthony Jr, Solomon, Samuel, Isaiah and Josiah, I love you today, tomorrow, and endlessly. My love grows for you and never fades you should know. I love you forever, I like you for always, as long as I am living my boys, my young kings you will be.

Precious Cargo

A mother's heart surrounds her kids and when these kids grow up, her heart surrounds the men they become. Words will never express the happiness I feel as I watch you blossom from a boy into a man. I gave birth to one of God's gift of life. A tiny baby boy, so precious and special. Little did I know a man is present in front of me, strong as a lion, courageous as a bear, and just as handsome as a pearl. Proud of you son, proud of all you have accomplished; keep pressing forward and never ever look back. Most of all be the best you, only you can be. I love you; I am your number one supporter.

Sons for life

It is with great honor I can call you son; for in the day where my head is low, you place a smile upon my face. A mother is fully satisfied when her sons look out for her; a mother is fully happy when her sons make her proud. I am so proud of the young men that you have become. Very detailed and very pleasant; although I may not say it all the time, I want you to know that I am most grateful for sons as you. I love you dearly, and am very proud of who each of you are. Continue your journey to be all that you can be, wavering nothing and allowing no one to come in between your future and happiness. Thank you, from the bottom of my heart, I appreciate you.

From the womb

Proud to say your mine, straight from my womb God's blessing was birthed. It's never enough to say I love you, but action speaks louder than words. I am so grateful that you my son have become the man you are today. Keep on pressing on, never look back, for the blessing comes in your persistence alone. Leave the haters behind you, for its not important what they think. The most important thing is that you my son are happy and well each day. I love you today, tomorrow, and for my lifetime.

Dedicated to Anthony Jr

Chosen

It is with great joy I hold your life in my hand. The moment I heard your cry, my love for you grew. I knew my responsibility would be great. A man of God has been born; I must cherish this life at hand. My son I will forever be here for you, when you fall my love will catch you. Your mistakes will guide you and lessons learned will mold you. Know your worth, know your calling and allow no one to steal your gift away. I am proud of you, proud to see you walk into your purpose. I love you now and forever more, my bundle of joy.

Dedicated to Solomon

Arrival

It is time, the baby is here; perfecting the space for this special one. Conditioning and strengthening, the battle has just begun. Anointed and called, this one alone. Great deal of pressure involved; See me through; I must guard against the spirits who long to destroy this being. Man child, your born; your cry is release knowing your life has just begun. I took my breath and with that wind, I will carry you. I will keep you close to me as best I could. Cover your heart for many want what you have been given. Worthy son, you must know you are; no one comes close to out smarting, out doing you. Your first step you have taken and now you run; I await the moment when a baller you will become. Keep that fight that you had from day one. I will love you from your first breath until the day I take my last breath.

Dedicated to Samuel

Unique

Where did the time go, from birth to present, my joy has grown! Proud of the young man that you have become. As I watch each day, my smile grows within; for I am certain that you Isaiah will one day be great. Your potential grows and your greatness exceeds most beyond the boarders and to the moon, you will one day be everything you hope and more, everything you desire to be. Your mind is focused and your goals are complete. Do not hesitate, do not fret do not fear; be the you that only you can be for no one will ever replace you nor take your courage away. Remain strong and never cease the fight, push through, follow through, and focus on the prize.

Dedicated to Isaiah

Completed

A tiny being held close to my bosom; protection I give him for I know a life time of teaching will be provided. My little one, worry will cease from you; for mama has your best interest at heart. I see the path so great for you; a leader at heart so many will follow you. Keep your courage even as a young boy. For you Josiah will one day be a warrior the world has never known. Boldness and strength, they are your characters and patience and love will see you through. As you continue this journey of life, know that mama will support and keep you safe, and when your age reaches the point when you're a man, my love will continue as I release you for the world perfection.

Dedicated to Josiah

Double love

Double the trouble for the price of love. Would never take back the joy you bring me inside, from the womb to the young man, its all with great joy that I watch you grow into these two men and bloom inside. Your so great, unique in fact; your loved from the bottom to the top of my heart. I love you guys; you are perfect just the way you were meant to be.

Dedicated to Solomon and Samuel

Yours

It's never boring seeing you grow right before my eyes; from the moment I laid eyes on you, I knew my heart was yours. I may not say it often, I may not speak to you each day, but son of mine, I love you dearly. You make me proud and keep a smile on my face. We may not agree on everything, but our bond, our love, will always make it way back. I am sure, I am confident, that your greatness will forever remain.

Waken Breath

Its with great pleasure that you're my son; you make me proud and always keep me happy. My love for you will never fade nor will it ever be dismissed; with each waken breath, I sigh relief, knowing that another day with you, has been granted to me. To hear your voice, to see you smile, its all a blessing, and enough to survive. I am grateful, excited, and thankful, for you as my son. Keep your head up and keep on keeping on.

A Sister's Love Never Ends

Circle of love

The importance of love ones to carry you through; whether blood or not it makes no difference to me. You are my circle my immediate ones in fact; I have grown to love you and trust you without a doubt. I am open to the fact that I can speak without hesitation, I can open up and not worry about the judgmental attitudes, or belittling spirits. It took a lot from me to say certain things but the fact that it was never thrown at me speaks louder to me. Our bond is greater than I could imagine; our bond has connected and locked into place. I know for a fact that when I fall one of you ladies will be there to catch me, and if one of you fall, I will catch you for sure. I have poured out my life before and when it was taken and mashed up, I climbed inside a bottle and never came out. The time with you ladies is always great; I feel so free, so special inside. I have no worries, I do not fret or frown, I am at peace and relaxed for I know my circle has me. I am glad that I have sisters who care for me, who will always be there.

Sisters of mine

It's a day full of life, for the biggest joy comes knowing that I have sisters in this life. Someone to talk to, laugh with and even cry with. Sisters are a blessing in disguise for me. I cherish you my sisters for you make life easier and smoother; you make my questions seem important and you cause the guards to fade. Your laughter fills my heart with joy within, and your presence secures any fears inside. I love you my sisters, I mean that for life; there's only one place I would rather be and that is being your life indeed. I may struggle and I may fall; this I know for sure that you won't let me die. You have my back even when so far away and the deepest of thoughts you make sense of it for me Sisters, thank you for being you, sisters thank you for caring so much, sisters I love you today, tomorrow, and beyond any other.

When sisters display love

Sister may sound so regular, but when you think about the role and the person in that role, the role the word sisters becomes more defined. My sisters are the best in the world, no matter how far or how near, we keep in touch to ensure each is ok. We send lots of love from a distance and when brought together our love completes each one. We are unique inseparable beyond words. I am grateful for my sisters who have proven faithful throughout the years. In the good and the bad, the bond we have will never break. I am proud of all my sisters; I love you to life.

Precious gift

Sisters are a precious gift; they remain faithful even when life seems to way us down. Sisters have your back you see and no matter what, their always just a phone call away. Sisters are God sent and every female can not be a sister; it takes the best of the best to really love unconditionally. My sisters bring my load down and encourage me when I am saddened. The one word I have describe my sisters is love. Sisters are the perfect tool for a winter storm for they will warm you up. Sisters are important because they help make you better. Sisters are warm and welcoming and very distinct. One must never take for granted the blessing a sister brings especially when a sister has a gift of love to give. They come in a small package with large entrance. Sisters are those who go out their way to see you through and make you comfortable. They are those who will hear you when no one else will. My sisters are number one!!

Enough

Its never enough to say I love you. To text or call on a daily basis. It's never enough to say please or thank you. What matters most is how you react to the person you say you love. How you treat the person who has been there for you. See, for me love is deeper than words and action. It's a lifestyle to appreciate those we love. Go out our way to accommodate, assist, and relieve our love ones. When I fall down on my knees and pray, I always thank God that I have sisters I know I could count on. From the inside out I want to say I love you dearly. You are the best sisters a sister can have. You're my best friends, the ones I can depend on. Thank you!!

What! A Sister?

When I think of a sister I think of pureness with no spots because she is perfect. When I think of a sister I think of consistency because every day her love remains. When I think of a sister I think of patience because whenever I need her, she is always there, with no hesitation just her love. When I think of a sister, I think of you because indeed you are a sister to me indeed. A sister is a sense of security when all else as failed. A basket of flowers to help blossom the day. A sister is a voice who never stops speaking because the words are engraved in the heart. A sister is a sigh of release knowing that their love will forever remain. A sister is created by God because their shoulders are wider and thicker than no other.

Clever Love

It's never intentional to hurt the one we love, for we cover them with peace and safety. When you hurt, my sister, I hurt, and your tears become mine. We shall a bond that no one will break and the fact of this life is that blood is thicker than water. I cherish you in my life, and believe that you have my best interest at heart. I understand that some decisions seem so foolish and yet so strong. Let's talk about it, and figure it out; for this we have must never fade away. I love you for your loyalty, and your commitment; I love you because when no one else was, you my sister have always been. You provided that shoulder to cry on, and that ear to listen. I am sorry I broke your heart, and caused the tears to drop. I will not push you away nor will I dismiss your thoughts. For what's more important to me is our friendship at large. We may not agree on everything, but I, my sister will always be there for you, as you are for me. Thank you for being you and loving so hard and caring unconditionally.

Thick and thin

When a friend becomes more than a friend, its important to treasure their every moment. My sister you are family to me, you have been there through thick and thin, been there through my ups and my downs. Today is the day to celebrate you, for who you are; that great woman, that amazing friend, the best mother your children will ever experience. You are the perfect you; I appreciate you; I love you, and most of all my sister, I treasure you. Thick & thin is our model, no one to come between us, sisters for life.

A brother's touch

Kept covered

Although not a young girl any more, I know that the questions asked, are to keep me covered. You may be so far but your heart is always near. You keep in touch and make sure that as your sister, you continue to display your protection. One may come and go, but I must say, my brother will always remain up close.

Family Ties

Families love

Family, the one thing in life that will never be up for sell. The bond is deep, our hearts are unique and most of all, no one will ever come between you and me.

Family, those who have each other's back and never allow for one to trip nor fall. To catch each one as we see fit before the fall.

Family, those who know us inside and out; those that will stand beside you through thick and thin. Those that won't speak against you come what may; it's this family bond that keeps us together and, in this circle, called love we remain for life. No one perfect, no one judging, it's this family that we are, that keeps us strong.

Love you family

Bonded

What's in it for the family to come together and love so hard. When others are fighting and not getting along; this family here draws closer each day and distance I may add never builds a bridge. We are like fire spreading throughout; where others wonder how could this family be so tight. I want what they have and need their love. It is our bond, our blood that runs deep inside for love. We are the waves that crosses millions, we are those voices that many imagined impossible. We are the family that prays together; therefore, will forever stand together.

Broken, Never Destroyed!

Whisper

Silenced wind and storm around, can't you see, I am trying to climb? The walls are slippery, the rain has caused such a mess around. I still return to climb some more. I am not defeated; I have not been conquered; just a small set back from before. The storm is raging causing a scene; everything around me is collapsing so quickly. Yet I refuse to throw in the towel, I refuse to give in to defeat. I am a champion, a winner inside; no one will take my victory away. I am determined to fight to the end. I may fall sometimes, I may even rest; but at the end, I will no longer give in. I am a silent storm, ready to rage, I have had enough, there's no turning back. I will press, pull and push; I will do what is needed to break through these walls. My hands are slippery, my body is aching, my head is hurting, but still I fight. To the end I will go, determined to win; to the end I will go, expecting a victory.

A frozen relief

Rejected, abandoned, left to die; bearing the shame that life has brought. Afraid, frozen in time, not knowing whether or not my life would prolong. I have carried this burden long enough; I have haltered this pain inside. Free, my life has become for bondage as broken, heartache rebuked, neglection expired for I am anew. Embarrassed no longer for I know that my life means more than the breath I take. Captured my memories, no longer holding me back; I have embraced this freedom that above has poured on me. Stronger, wiser, lovable in fact; engaged in wisdom to know my right from wrong. No longer this child kept imprisoned so long; my chains have broken; my wings have finally extended.

Steal

It's a fight every day it seems, a fight to breathe, a fight to live, a fight to conquer freedom. Aggression, I have my share; no longer desiring aggression for it frightens me. I only asked for happiness for once in my life; to be able to experience peace. Aggression is too much for me to handle for all around me, storms are raising. I thought for a moment it would be okay; silly me to think that I would be able to sleep away the pain. Another night without sleep, for I can not bare the pain I feel. It is a shame what this creates; pain for me, pain for others. It's been too good to be true; my guard was down, vulnerable to all. If anything, I refuse to share my pain, for the hurt inside me was like no other. I don't want aggression, all I wanted is to live; I don't want aggression its too much to keep. Fear crept in; I am determined to shake it off, the reality is the fear to trust has overtaken me.

Battle

It may not be with guns and knives; perhaps not even with a fist or slap. The battle begins within oneself to grow, to glean, to desire a change. Curled up in a fetus position I am, just waiting for my chance. A chance at success, happiness, I hope; a chance at peace, deliverance expected. The weapon is stronger, for it is the mind; a weapon of uncertainty, perhaps confusion. As time progress position changes, fetus position, no more. I scream, I kick, I push and beat; it is my turn, so wait until I burst. Like a butterfly coming out of the cocoon; like a baby coming out of the womb. Brand new, I want to be, whether childish, whether silly, I just want a new life, new chance at peace.

Can you taste it?

Acquiring a taste for the untouched, unnoticed, unfamiliar lifestyle. What can I say, but I am ready, ready to take it to the next level! Freedom is calling my name, finally; a taste of courage, a taste of pride. Look at me now, a Queen at heart; born with struggles, pain around me, beauty is vain when it doesn't come from within. I am more than just ordinary; I have risen to the challenge. I have made my presence known, no one to slow me down. Queen you say, yes that is me. I am worth every minute, every second in fact. I am important, I am a jewel, more precious then silver, better than gold. I have made it past the haters, I have made it past those that said I never would.

Acquiring a taste for the untouched, unnoticed, unfamiliar lifestyle. What can I say, but I am ready, ready to take it to the next level! Freedom is calling my name, finally a taste of independence, a taste of success. No longer wavering, no longer hesitant. I am coming out of the shell I was so long encaged in. For a queen has managed to create a path, unfamiliar yet safe for her.

New Day

Careful touch of what's to come, over it, not nearly. I feel a silent calm storm beginning to rage. I know its weird perhaps even crazy, but I truly think that a new pain will rise. I try to remain level headed, to think positive no matter what. Thus far al I have seen is disappointments, after disappointments. I sit on the side of the bed and I think to myself, what will today bring? Will I have to be afraid; will I have to stand on my toes; what will today look like with raging waters all around me. The bottom line, I begin to stand, to think, is that for me? I plan my day; my day turns out the way I make it. No one has the power over me, to determine the way my day will turn out. Perhaps there will be trails, tribulation to cross, but at the end of the day, my day is what I make of it. I will not allow the struggles of life to get me down, no not I. I have been down for so long; I plan on getting up and moving forward. I may be down, but not defeated, I may be weak, but not conquered; I will arise as I have before; I will make sure I am better then where I was before. This storm around me will not defeat me; I will make it yet another day ahead.

Twisted

Tornado around me, bringing everything down and causing the walls to fall. Scary image, no one to hold me, left to bare it the best I could. The sky has darkened, the clouds have changed; in a twister I believe I am in. Going around and around with no way out, the trauma of pain has hit again. A constant motion to bring me down, my hands are reaching for a solid fixture. No grip to hold, no exit, I can't escape. Tornado hits in every way possible; the sky is fallen; my will has stopped. I watch, as in the middle of this turmoil I stand; I sit for a second to analyze this mission. Do I stay or do I go, do I run from this pain that's causing all this chaos, or do I stay and face the tornado alone? Am I equipped to rebound from this? Have I gotten the tools needed to stand on my own? My hands are weak, my mind confused, weary I am, left to decide on my own. My feet are heavy no longer able to stand, how can I move without a pace of my own? Disabled, detached, disconnected I have become. No heart for it has been snatched, no feelings they have been abused, no emotions, I am cold as brew. What must I say, what must I do? A diamond in disguise, rotten from this storm, broken in pieces, no one able to mend me. A diamond has been crushed, pieces are scattered, some small, but many pieces are large. I find a glow, even just an ounce of hope; one piece is unique which stands on its own. I stand again, with hope holding me, bringing me up out the tornado that took a hold of me. My pieces are slowly coming together, the diamond I know I am will one day raise again. It's still spinning, it's still turning, however, I am no longer in the middle. I have come out of the midst of chaos; isolated from fools, fake and all. Shut out from the world around me, no one really knows me. They see me now and think she has no control of the situation at hand. She will not overcome; how can she, she has no one. I am here to say that hope has carried me, hope has given me that second chance. Hope has provided a sense of security. Where my pains are wrapped in hope; all my hurts, hope has taken. I am no longer afraid, no longer controlled by the terror that had me bound. Diamond, I am, filled with potential, who knows my story, who knows my path. Hope has come to my rescue, to lead me to a calmer place. Forget those who troubled me, I will not allow the same mentality to grip me and control me. Hope has come, has taken the jewel that so desperately needed a peace of mind. This jewel, this diamond, so precious and fragile. I will conquer, I will rule; I will take control of my life alone. I will bare the pain, the struggles, the hurts, the disappointments. Hope has come, taken this diamond, this precious cargo, so fragile, so unique; and has equipped her with the power, stamina, courage, and confidence to rule the world as such should. Don't bow down now; don't run to me; don't take a second look for I guarantee, I won't. Hope has caused me to build the walls with my hands, to guard my heart as I only can. What now? You fool, don't second guess me again for I am done. Look and hear, I come out the dark, my glow so pure; my words well-spoken as I stand higher and above than most. I have made it; I did not give up. Stronger and wiser, better than before.

Taken

Never a right time to throw in the towel; never a right time to walk away and leave it all behind me. The moment is fragile, the time is right; no need to second guess the thoughts that flood my mind. Its freedom I need; freedom I deserve. Too many years of pain, heart-aches; disappointments; too many years of unhappiness. Fed up with all, family, friends, I have scratched it all out; my bill wiped clean, a new beginning I take. No one will ruin my heart, mind, soul again; no one will control me, I control myself. Stepping out one foot at a time, a little afraid of the journey ahead. My time has come, my challenge, I have won, my life is worth the fight in spite of the pain. I have taken a chance of a lifetime, to be independent, bright and successful. I've made up my mind to take my life back; to reach for the stars; to conquer even one. I feel good; strong and wise; I feel an inch of strength come over my body. I am a winner; survivor in fact; my story so long, but I will take the time to share. My life is worth living to the fullest and even beyond.

Slaved

Penetrated deep inside; my anger rages all around. I have not learned to deal with pain, to ease away my hurts. My past hunts me; controls me; abuses me; many sleepless nights I have, wishing it to be different. A female, inspired by pain; can you imagine all that's enslaved? For so many years I have kept it in; no sharing; not letting go. No one concerned with my feelings at hand; never really dealt with the demons that rang. And now as a grown woman, I have been forced to flash back the reality of life. My arms are pulling, my feet are slipping, my head is spinning, my stomach is turning. All of the tension that I suppressed has risen to the occasion. Forced to recognize that in life I must deal with these demons at hand. Afraid for a moment to take full control; to really flash back and uproot what's been dormant so long. In a quiet space I need to be; to really appreciate that the hurts; the pains, have made me different, shaped me for today. Difficult time, I experience trying to be a free woman indeed. Free to live; free to love; free to say and do what I want. What may come natural to another becomes difficult for me as I have been a certain way for so long. No worries, I will pull through; I will be sure to increase in knowledge and level on my own. It has been established; it has been contracted; I will be born again; given another chance at life for sure.

Eagles wings

Upon wings I sit all day; strength I have; courage I lack. Release is coming, I sense it in the air. I can not bare this pain alone; wounded and abused; mistreated; confused. I need these wings to stretch as far and deep as possible. I no longer want the routine, the rut of living just to make it through. To wake the same and be the same; these wings I have developed; have allowed me to stretch a little at a time; to reach deeper than before; to imagine and practice new life with happiness. I want to fly above the world. I want to go where I have never been before. To stretch my wings and breathe again; to venture to a destiny that has been waiting for me since the beginning of time. Don't just sit there and watch me fade; don't allow me to dissolve and decay. Speak a word; reach out and grab me; hold me up; don't let me fall. I have been wounded way too long. Quench my thirst; provide healing for my heart. These wings I have; I will fly again. Believe in me so that I myself can believe in me. Don't let go; don't fade away; don't allow me to be a shadow in the night and a vision during the day. Allow me to spread these wings; to stretch and go wherever I please. Trust in me; I can do this; I will fly again; I will conquer and sit in my throne of happiness, peace, joy, and satisfaction. I will fly;

my wings will spread wide. I will be all that potential will allow. At the end, victorious I will become.

Attacked

When the attacks get stronger and deeper, the mind reacts with stress and overwhelming pressure. It's never enough to cling to a string, never enough to cry uncontrollably. Pain is worth the hurt, tears is worth shedding, for the end result is better. My mind spins as troubles come, appearing to never do the right thing at all. I feel the pressure of life's story unfolding, causing me to break. I receive the static from every corner, north, south, east and west; every passing moment causes me to flinch. Not knowing what would happen next; I smile and keep my hurts and pains hiding so as to not unlock my feelings and let anyone in. I smile for fear of disappointment; I smile for lack of control. I don't want anyone to know that this pain is too much to carry on my own. I try to keep myself busy best I can, so as to not think about the chaos at hand. A moment to sit is a moment of hurt, which brings the emotions flowing fast as can be. Is anyone there? Can you figure me out? I am really dying inside, really empty. I don't desire this path of routine; I really regret my past experience. I realize I am not perfect just trying to make it the best I can. Excuse me for a moment for it seems my life at pause. Reflection of pain I reach out no one to hold. I know I am something to one, just don't really know exactly the details at all. My life's a mystery, getting away from it all. Anew, afresh, I just desire to be. To be brand new and better for no one but me. I am no punk, no wimp at all; my struggles will one day pass and into the light I will stand. Tougher than ever, a warrior in fact. Ready for combat; ready to last. I am precious you see, too important to pass. To cling to life like no body's business. This too shall pass; my mind will be made anew; one moment will cause the entire pain to lose. I will climb and crawl, I will fight with my all, knowing that one day my life will be worth it all.

Powerless

Cut by words that never cease, wondering why I have been the chosen one. Not good enough, no way smart enough. Beautiful far from it; words have damaged me, taken my very being away. Trap in a situation that seems impossible to fix. Not feeling loved, appreciated or even wanted. Charged with a crime so heavy that my life will always revolve around it. Not a perfect being you see, just lived the life everyone around me wanted to see. Fraud? For sure; I only managed to create an illusion for everyone to see. I refused to be questioned for fear my struggle, my sadness will come out. I just allowed the time to row, and my pain to unfold. Scared and weary too tired to go on. It's only for a moment that the damage will hold, my memories swirling out of control. Got it, I am finally above it, I will pursue my life for happiness to earn.

Alone

Abandoned and set aside for loss; left to manage these feelings, emotions all alone. Where do I look, where do I turn, I have never been in this place before? My heart is crushed, my mind is discarded; alone, nervous, scared o my. I am in a dark place, never been before; melting away and dying from the inside out. Energy snatched; my words are shut. I am looking for some release, but reality is, it will never come. I am not perfect nearly close to it. I just wanted happiness, at least what I envisioned it would be. A roller coaster ride, never getting off, just riding in a circle going as fast as I can. Tired and dizzy, I feel I have reached a place where never again will I trust anyone. I thought I could manage, I thought I could win. Realty is the fight has been over for I've ended my fight; I've thrown in the towels to vanish; I wish I could. To perish beyond no other, and carry this shame alone; how could this happen? What I thought would last, has ended because of a shift in behavior. I have carried this pain long enough; I will not carry it any longer. Looking for an exit to come face to face; to try afresh a new life on my own. I will make happiness appear again just on my terms; I am more than enough to make it on my own. I don't want another being to replace what I've lost. I don't want another being to try and mend my heart. There is no possible way to really express my pain to some. Words are not heavy enough; this pain I have I pray one day will go away. To be replaced by confidence, love of myself, and freedom to live. I have tried so hard to enclose those emotions, to hide how I feel, and now I have reached the point of no return. Isolated, alone, I want to be; fix? Impossible for a broken vase must go to waste. Broken in so many ways, explaining will not help, but I believe I will raise one, day if not I am done.

Soaring above

Finally flying away, high above the skies beyond; no one near, no one to catch me. I float on the clouds never look back. A new day, a new adventure; fear over takes me as high above I soar; for untouched territory I enter with no one near. It is my time to shine, I can do this on my own; this marks the first day of forever for me. I don't know what to expect, I don't know what's on the other end; but one thing true, is that I can fly. I am capable of so much, I never knew; I am starting to find myself, like a new born babe. Learning to crawl, to stand and walk in fact; on my own venturing my ties. I am perfect in my own little way. I acknowledge for this is final, I am somebody. Surrounded by clouds, white as snow, my beginning, my fresh start, my adventure I claim. It's overwhelming I must say, I feel so alone, scared, just want the norm. Inside of me something breaks out, it's been hiding, doormat for so long and now the taste of freedom I have. Floating, no worries at hand, will I make it another day, far fetch inside. That's the least of my worries for I am miles away, can't catch me now. Rest I have gripped and peace I have taken, for safety in the clouds, hidden away from the pain. I am stronger, I am closer to my destiny, I never thought it would follow. I would have never thought a day would come when my chains have been released, where my past unleash. I close my eyes, new air I breath, I give a sigh; relief I feel. Floating, allow me to stay just for the moment in this fresh air inside. All around fluffy clouds, which provides a sign of patience, knowing my time is near. Thank you clouds for holding me up, for given me peace I desired inside. Thank you, air, I can breathe again, a sigh of relief has come to me.

A Faithful transition

Imagine the day where relief will be caught, when my sorrow will turn to joy and my anger to peace. My bitterness will be a distant memory and I will fly away to a better place; I will be happy, I will feel joy, I ill be at peace with myself and others. A place where my tears will cease and laughter replaced. I will be able to be myself with no questions asked and my character never questioned again. A place where I will be accepted for me, for who I am and all I have to offer. I await that day where I breakthrough; where my pain and hurts are so easily forgotten. When I fly to this place, I expect my life to be a fresh. I will rise now, stay strong, too soon will this imagination become my reality. I will remain calm, its okay to scream and pounce; cry my tears and angrily hit the wall; throw a bottle perhaps two; let it all out and relax. I have come this far and have caused shackles to break. I have shaken the very foundation of those that controlled me; see its not me that fallen, it's really those that have hurt me who are uncertain about the next move. I have created a greater cause and broken the trend of this life. So, this place of peace already exists, it has always waited me so patiently. I was stuck and unable to reach it; but my eyes are open and going towards it; I have become somebody, that I myself do not know. Those around me question me, but the very ones that talk to me, do not understand just how hurt I have become. It is easy for those to dismiss this pain, but for me it is how I have lived. It is not my end, just the beginning of what's to come. I will encounter relief and my freedom will be unleashed.

Finding Hope

Above, haven't fallen for once; feeling better and not as worried as I was past days. Hope has come to my rescue yet again; hope never fails, never leaves me alone. I felt as if I did not deserve hope, but hope clings to me and gives me a spark, even a glow. It is indeed a blessing to have hope and believe in something even if worthy I am not. My smile is authentic, even inspired; at a better place I find myself, hope has come through again. I was weakened, depressed, and shattered, hurt by the ones around me; alone I felt as if no one quite understood my pain, my sorrow in fact. But I have realized that it is not what people do to me that determines my success, my happiness at that. I must stand in the midst of this turmoil and cause my feet to be planted, solid as can be. Unmovable, unstoppable, unshakeable I must become. I hold hopes hand knowing with hopes help I will make it; I will stand as strong as ever, never to be taken down again. I must fight, for a warrior at heart I am. Stronger than I think; even stronger than others perceive. Who am I kidding, but myself alone; I am somebody, I have worth above all others. I am important, for I am satisfied with me.

Mirrored by my love

Allow me to float for just some time, my mind to fluctuate all around. I was crippled for so long, where was I, I dare not try. Captured inside, whom did I become? Who was I, if I was inside? My mouth was silenced; my cry was shut away; laughter never seemed to rely on me. Happiness and peace were so buried inside; encamped and wavered for so long. Allow me to float, extend and breathe; my release has come and now I am free. I am free to dance my legs are strong; free to laugh my mouth has opened; free to think my thoughts alone; for the bottled have open and my freedom has exploded. Mirrored by the love of just one, finally living my life endured. Floating with health, life, and meaning; finally arrived with peace beside me.

Do you trust me?

What is trust if doubt is present? It is deeper than the ocean, for issues with trust must have appeared before. Questioned about the little things when in reality its been smooth sailing. I got it; I finally reached that point where I will not receive negativity just because. If by chance you doubt me, then the walking you need to be. I excuse myself from this roller coaster, for in a whirlwind I feel I am in. I will not take down another time, for right now it is not the right thing to do. I am tired, sleepless nights I have viewed. You constantly put me down when your upset and annoyed; but when its all peachy and smiles you lift me up. Sorry sir, I am done, I excuse myself from this wreck. I no longer desire to feel like I am always at fault; my mind is clear and my heart at peace. At least I know that this time around for sure it wasn't me.

Purpose in change

There are many who can't find their way, no guidance given no path provided. Left to figure it out alone, and make do with what one has. Tired of the same results; going around and round spinning out of control. Mindset must change, new direction must be desired. We are not alone, raised thinking that loneliness is accepted. There's a being greater than this, that provided the guidance needed for change to occur. We may not agree nor like what's given; but at the end, there must be purpose within the change. Finally, here, do I turn right or is left my path? Do I look backward or is forward where my life should be? Decisions, decisions, now look at what's different. Every time I look back my past followed me. When I go left it seems that the hurts present themselves again, when I move right, all the anger and frustration I felt comes crashing down. This is new, for not once I have moved on; through the path right in front of me. Uncertain, unfamiliar, uncontrollable it is. For if I walk ahead to the life I've never had, I will not know what to expect. Would I get to experience change whether good or bad, not sure? I'll take the risk and follow my heart, for all other roads set me back aside. Newness inside for brighter this road has become. My past has vanished and new life, new hope has risen. I have started over, refreshed inside I am. Walking into my own place dressed with my likens and mine alone. Breath of fresh air to wake with freedom and peace; to move as I please without the bondage near. I have made it; a new life to build, hope never gave up on me, I, just me, had to find this road alone. I must say with all the wait, patience and desires, there is a purpose within the change desired.

Peace of mind

Walking with my head held high, never looking down, even if in error. I walk with confidence, I stagger nothing; when I walk, I leave a trail. Many ask, what's wrong with her? Boy I have never seen her upset. I need what she has; is it a man? Perhaps, she is rich. I kindly smile, never looking back; I struggle at times, but no one will ever know. For the queen in me, acknowledges the fact that no one has their life together but God. My daily routine consists of a thank you prayer to God, for waking me up in the morning. Followed by a shower and some food. My day is consumed with duties and responsibilities, but I, I never lose myself in the midst. I take care of me. My hair is done, my nails look neat, my attire, well what can I say, is fly every time. My smile is lit and for the record, God put that smile on me. I may not be perfect; I may not be rich; but if you must know for sure what's wrong with me, I have peace of mind you see.

Why?

You chased me for a while then it all stopped. You cared for me and whispered all I wanted to hear. You misled me, you caused me to trust you and believe in you. I became close to you and needed your presence in all. You knew you had me and used that to hurt me, manipulate me and most of all to cause me to think that it was all me and never you. You grew apart from me as I began to draw close to you. I opened up completely while you, you remind closed within. You knew everything about me, an open book I became; while I, I hoped and prayed that you would open as well. you crushed me, destroyed me, and broke me deep inside. You left me to die alone in despair. Vulnerable, hurt, desperate for answers. Silence you gave, silence I received. My head buried; my soul confused. All I wanted, was taken for granted; melted by lies, deceit, complaints, which I,

I believed. My pureness taken yet again I can't believe. My life for granted, it laid in unbelief. Proven so painful this life that's suppose to grow strong; claiming my sincerity, leaving me with pain. Cutting my core, leaving me breathless to cling to the pores. I've vanished, I've lost the one thing I cherished deeper than all. My heart snatched, removed from the sincerity it once knew. Complications and disaster have followed and my pain grows inside weaker I become. Its not my past that hurt more, but my present which stands in the way. You monster, you creature, demon in fact; you took my life, my everything and took advantage of it. You knew that I would do anything and more. You guided me astray and caused me to fall. You turned your back on me when I needed you the most. You charmed me and took, took, and took it all away. Leaving me with nothing but hurt and pain. The good memories submerged for the bad has outweigh it all. The curse of being young and naïve to all; what kind of creature are you with no care in the world. What monster you turned out to be and just smile like you've won. A bastard, a demon, caved and masked by pride and selfishness. You claim your territory then slowly destroy it with greed and deceit. Leaving the territory alone as before. Its okay you see for at the end of the day I know for sure that I am a great woman, loving, beautiful, giving, kind, smart, confident, patient, and overall, I know I am one of a kind.

Angel

Powered by the force around me; being home feeling the freedom inside. Positivity surrounds me for my dear angel has come to visit. Waves are high and pure for sure; sand on my feet, allows me to feel the relief. Peaceful and calm, no one to stop me now; I am new, I have grown, no fears no worries inside. For I have made a commitment to keep a smile no matter what. Its all around this peace I feel; never felt this calm as I feel right now. Preparing for greatness which has been stirred inside me. I have been blessed to move past my pain, my hurts, my struggles. Looking back no more, for distraction I wave them good bye. Powered by the force around me; being home feeling the freedom inside. Positivity surrounds me for my dear angel has come to visit. New meaning of life I have gained; there is no limit to dreams that must be brought to life.

Manifested within

The wind is blowing all around; waves tossing to and forth. I am steady, unmovable, untouchable with the passing of time. My legs perhaps are worn down, but my fight will never fade; perfect balanced with the waves and the wind, trying to take me out. I am here to stay, so wind blow another way; waves grow higher for the battle within will not push me away. I've been told that the waves the wind, will take me out, but watch as this queen fiercely fights and makes her way. They don't know the fight within, for when one says I can't, I know I must. Not given up, theses winds blow harder; tired I get but never given in. A day at a time, to build my strength, to push through these winds, the waves that do not bend. Headed my way no angle in its firm, the grip takes my breath, but finally I relax. On top of it all, the winds must go; waves must follow another day. For I sit alone, in my victory seat, never doubting, always knowing I had the strength within.

A Woman's Fight

Tired

It's such a shame that a woman has to go through so much pain, so much frustration. It's never enough for a woman to just live her life with happiness and peace. Story? Never enough, as long as she has responsibilities, she is never really free. Everyone around will give their opinion, but the one opinion that should count doesn't count. Come on Women, lets change the strategy; come on women, lets make the best of it. Considered as weak, I get you see, for men so long have been told they are it. Provide for the family, and pay the bills; make babies; and make sure the woman depends on you. Well women times have changed, it's a brand-new day, we can survive with taken care of ourselves. Struggle, never over, lets make best with what we have; confusion will set in but its up to us to walk out. We have power deep down inside us. We will cry and even stress, but women we must never dethrone ourselves.

Overwhelmed

Feeling a little overwhelmed, for constant nagging occurs, there is no rest for me right now. There's always something being said; I am one person you see; how can I handle all of this? To the brink I feel me raising, desiring to be left alone is what I am longing. A break from life, a break from the responsibilities that hold us captive. So much expected from just one person; it's expected to forgive, forget, and go along. It's a misunderstanding you see, for the life of me cannot go along with foolishness. I am wiser than all of that; stronger then imagined; I have an unseen plan; my freedom foreseen. I have fallen a little short, but by the end of the day, I will be back on my feet fighting until the end.

Bundle

Been in the bottom way too long; my self esteem shattered by the one I gave my life to. I packaged my feelings and buried my emotions. I left the side of strength and chattered words of pretense. I carried the weight of the world on my shoulder and allowed my energy to be removed. My head was bowed down for so long, that I lost myself within. I hid behind the presence of control and allowed my surroundings to make me. I walked in the shoes of others and tried to fill the spot I never wanted. I dressed according to the book and set aside my desires for those around me. My smile faded as I no longer desired the fake but wanted what was real. My eyes finally open to the reality that life is suppose to look like. A woman cherished will flourish; loved and cared for, will blossom. A woman encouraged will be determined; a woman with courage will succeed no matter what comes her way. That woman is me, for so long I walked to the beat of control, I took the neglect just to make myself important. Dying inside, looking for a release for peace. I took the mask of and now everyone is seeing me; they do not agree, nor accept me, won't appease. There's something I must do to become all I can; to embrace my greatness and potential I must conquer. Shunned upon for so long, embarrassed to make a mistake and afraid to disappoint others. All done with it, all completely discarded. I will not fade; I will not die; I am more than a woman with solution so strong. Stronger than most because I have endured so much; lies after lies; I believed but never knew the truth until now. I will become victorious one way or another. My dreams that died years ago will once again raise and create success for me. I am stronger today then past days apart. I claim my prize for its me that makes the difference occur. I will fight, determined to win; no need to weep for pain has been released. New found power enclosed withing, will not allow no one to push me away. I am alive, my inner man has risen again. This time so different for wiser I have become. I am important, I am attractive, I am a woman once buried, alive I will remain. Watch out world a newness begins, no longer shy, no longer humbled, but more than enough to make it this far.

Defined

I am not defined by what I do; tied down and made to feel less than a woman. My worth stems greater than words that have broken me in time past. A wonder to many, for few words I speak, but my presence intimidates. Intelligent, profound and beautiful, so sweet; characterized by commitment and loyalty alone. Quick to follow hesitant to lead. Once I gain the momentum to lead, I lead with passion, truth, and strength. I am a warrior at heart not looking to bend; against all odds my life has been, and now those that doubted me are afraid of my potential. I have left behind my past, hurts and pains; looking to build on my strength that has risen. Amazed with the courage I have gained, the freedom that was hid. Never really examining the greatness within; a wonder to many, disguised for a moment. At the end, flattered you will be; I am a mystery, not easily figured out; I am an open book, nothing hidden within. I am but that woman that came out of the bondage that held me tight, no longer there, a treasure unleashed for the world to see.

Peaceful place

I think I am at a place where I have accepted my situation, and now I am doing me working on, and strengthening me; being that mother that I need to be. In a dark place long enough, struggling with acceptance and wondering why me? Why am I not good enough, why was I pushed to the side? I woke up early today and reflected on who I am in God; so, it doesn't matter that my chapter ended, because a new book has started. Walking beside darkness, hand in hand at that; a moment of silence where it seemed too much. I had to shake it all off or gone with the wind I would become. I can't say I am healed completely, but what I know is that I feel stronger today. A lighter load I carry, for I let go of cargo I couldn't change. I did not think for once I would get here, I thought sure that my life would just drift away with no meaning at all. I thought I was worthless perhaps even nothing. But with this wind I felt this morning, I am okay, and accepted there is a new book being written on my life. Its not what others want for me or even what they expected of me; but I first had to learn that happiness is not in a man, rather in God. So, I am proud to say I have let go of many things, and this new book will reveal my strength I possess inside. I will be that mother, that woman, so many doubted me. I am living today because I made a decision, one that would change life course forever, and now I am at peace with myself, knowing I will make it.

Secret feeling

Behind my smile is a hurting heart, that's been through so much and now attacks still rise. Behind my laugh I am falling apart; I am so tired of the routine. I smile and act like everything is okay, but I just hold back the tears and walk away. I pick myself up determined to make it, although inside it hurts like hell. To open up then be refused if the freedom of speech that only one has. Is there purpose behind an opinion? Does that opinion really matter if at the end of the day control is what's desired? Who am I, but another woman who has been shattered and broken away. I have come too far to be held back from those who do not quite understand me; allow me to explain who I am in a proper and professional way. I was that child that no one really wanted; was despised because I was different. I was that teenager that was taken advantage of, but yet I rise. I was that young mother who made a decision of life and combining the two. I regret so much but I cannot take it back. As a woman I was degraded and for so long silenced inside. As a mother my rights were snatched and all I could do was be a slave in my own home. As I slowly opened up and blindfolds fell off, I became stronger and wiser. So much love I want to share, but deep inside afraid I become. For inside of me, I do not want to become any other than myself. Even now my days are counted, my struggles are intensified; nonetheless, I am victorious. I have taken a small detour, but now my path is clearer. I am not a punk, but confident inside, I do not desire to be lose where experience comes and go; instead, I treasure my life and acknowledge that my life matters, much more than a single night. My life has worth far beyond riches and gold. My life is a treasure, my body a jewel. All I ever wanted was to be loved for me alone; I do not ask for much, I know. For as an independent woman I will continue this journey and remind on point. I am stronger than before, wiser in a sense, for foolishness will not cross my path. So, for those who are confused, please do not be for although life has its way of challenging me, those challenges I will overcome.

Beauty inside

The warmth and fuzziness that causes one to freeze; the smiles that develop once acceptance has been defined. It is you indeed that must rise, higher than the valley and deeper than the sea. No obstacle to hard to prohibit your growth; no hurdle to high to obstruct your dream. There's potential in all; greatness to be uphold. Believe in yourself if no one around you believe in you. For me, I, you, we, are our own worst enemies; always critiquing ourselves, finding fault in all we do. Allowing the words of others to make or break our lives alone. Let's pause a moment, take a look in the mirror. Who do you see when faced one on one alone? You are greatness, despite the faults; you are significant, you bloom wherever you go. Our stories may not be similar, but at the end of the day, we must believe the same. Believe that we matter, I matter you see, make no mistake for what we go through makes us a warrior at heart. We must fight, we must push, we must continue with our lives, no matter what we go through. Remember, you, me, we, are a beauty inside.

Who would have known?

To every step there's a purpose, a wonder that linkers behind. My silence unexplainable. Behind closed doors I would rather be, for its safer to be alone then to fade away into someone else's shadow. I am greater, bigger than this. I am a mystery waiting to beam. No one can solve me, nor figure me out. A puzzle with pieces all over the board. I am one of a kind, not once have you heard or seen this before. Wiser than many, for years of suffering I have managed. My heart protected by the pain that was; slowly opening but now I've closed it. I've become my own queen, protecting myself inside. I won't allow no foolish whisper, or no lies to cause me distraction. I won't allow a simple smile to cause me to walk another path. I am focused, I am myself. I am that beauty that would never allow. Abundance and flourishing above, I am that one that no one knew how. With patience, diligence, persistence and calmness; I've managed to grow past my pain and hurts; managed to blossom further than expected. I have come so far that to my eyes I wonder; but I know that it was I, me alone that made it. I purposed my heart, my soul, my mind, to make each day a lesson in disguise. I shed many tears away from all, but my smiles reveal the growth inside. No stopping me now, I should add, for in my mind, my heart, my soul, I can not be moved.

Refreshed

I have never felt the way I do; I have never experienced all this joy. I have managed to walk into who I am, and embrace myself completely. I am not ashamed of the woman I have become; confident and strong wavering nothing. Taken down no more, I have been renewed. Wiser today then I was before, queen of my world, the only one of its kind. I am not afraid to stray and try new things; I am brand new, a blessing that has waited long enough. I am myself, the winner of life, the storage of joy. Walking with my head held high, realizing that my freedom is on time. My walk reflects my confidence, my speech displays my education, my attire demonstrates my class, and my smile gives my peace away. I have never felt the way I do; I have never experienced all this joy. I have managed to walk into who I am and embrace myself completely. I am not ashamed of the woman I have become; confident and strong, wavering nothing at all. Taken down no more, I have been renewed.

Being True to yourself

Feelings, your feelings are valid; why would you think its not? It's your inner person, the very core of your soul. Your emotions, no one else can define. Feelings that consume one, whether weak or strong.

Emerged, engrossed, overtaken by it all. Believing that the feelings may never fade. Be in tone to you, for no one else can. You are unique inside, and you alone hold the key which unlocks. Feelings are categorized by those who surround us.

Gentle Flow

Listen to the river which flows from the heart. The sound of the waves you know rises; causing a calming within oneself. Letting go of the pain that was; this river flows beneath allowing me to walk on water and disrupting the drowning inside. Flow water flow, for my heart controls the direction it goes. Do not think for a moment that my guard has gone down, and that my pain has over taken me. I am better than that, stronger you should know, for unlike others, I see an end to the flow. The river is heavy, full of life above; and my heart is open to receive what it must. Taken the lesson learned from one heart break to the next, knowing that just as a river passes on, this too shall pass. My heart will mend, my direction will be clear. I will not fall nor will I break. For this river inside will flow, until it finds its end above.

A woman's desire

From birth, a little girl yawns for attention and protection; she needs affirmation to ensure that she is cared for. As a teenager she seeks for direction to guide her through. Decisions made are based on a simple guess and when failure hits she crumbles but tries again. The little girl, teenager, and adult, now desires to be loved unconditionally, and wishes to be held and understood. Every disappointment pushes her further and further away, and with every disagreement her heart closes to the world around her. Once her heart has been broken, she will never allow for another put it together. A woman will be her own strength and never apologize for being unique. At the end a woman sits and realizes that life has thrown her a mixture of things. Feelings; emotions; challenges; struggles; there all so overwhelming. This woman nonetheless, never gives up and never allows one to win over her. Although she may fall, I guarantee she will pick herself up and start again.

Exactly the same

I am who I say I am; whether a warrior who never gives up, or that worker who is faithful. There's a fight inside of me that never ceases, never fades. Disappointments come and go; but through it all I have managed to let them go. I am my own team even when no one wants to join me. I am my own team, even when no one selects me. Born alone, I will die alone; nothing is needed for lies I have heard. What I thought was real, ended up being a hoax.

I am who I say I am; whether a lover who always gives her all, or that queen that passes nothing along. I am my own, even when no one sees me for who I am. I am my own, even when doubts arise inside. I managed thus far and now I have learned that the best team to be on is my own; I will never let myself down, I will always stand by my side; even when life has turned its back on me. My deepest thoughts will never again be released; for not worthy of my feelings is all I get. I am okay, I will make it; for after all, I am who I say I am; I am a queen in my own way, a beauty that compared to no other. A mother who fights for her seed and a woman who has grown to its peak. I am perfect I my own way in fact.

Queen Bee

Is it enough to lay down your happiness for another person? Whose decision would it be to allow one to die, while the other has control? No one really knows the power invested inside; unless challenged and proven, doormat one remains. Captured by the very fear that has forbidden lives to live. Stop and pause for a moment, realize who you are. A queen at heart a beauty at birth; you are that woman that man envies because of the strength you hold. That woman that men wishes he has for eternity, for the faithfulness you bare. The way you walk, captures the eyes of many; the way you speak, impresses those around you. The attire you wear, amazes that man to stare. So, I ask again queen; is it enough to lay down your happiness for another person? Whose decision would it be to allow one to die while the other has control? As you stand tall, the haters will hate, and those around you will begin to bow. For there is none like you, who compares to the love you give, the compassion you share. Look around you, that lady that stares, she is confused about you. Not understanding how every day you manage your chores with a smile on your face; look around, you are that queen bee that for so long you were told you would never be. You have made it, you come so far; pick up your crown, lay it on your head, walk the red carpet for inside of you great things lay.

Frightened but relieved

That little girl curled up inside, afraid to come out, afraid venture in pride. The silliness that consumes her knowing that lie is full of joy. Desiring to experience he fullness of life and investigate for herself the details of love. This little girl blossoms so full and catches a break when true love appears. Amazed at what's at hand and questions fill her mind. Trying to make sense of it all; she throws in the towel and jumps right into the deepest feeling the deepest thought that consumed her being. Relieved and captured by this one that allows for love to flourish inside. Not a little girl any more, but the best woman inside she has become.